Read and Do Science
COLOR

Written by Melinda Lilly
Photos by Scott M. Thompson
Design by Elizabeth Bender

Educational Consultants

Kimberly Weiner, Ed.D

Betty Carter, Ed.D

Maria Czech, Ph.D
California State University Northridge

Rourke
Publishing LLC

Vero Beach, Florida 32963

Before You Read This Book

Think about these facts:

1. Do you see any colors when you stand in complete darkness? Why not?

2. What is your favorite color? Why is it your favorite?

The experiments in this book should be undertaken with adult supervision.

©2004 Rourke Publishing LLC

Photo Credits: page 5, courtesy of National Oceanic and Atmospheric Administration (NOAA)/Department of Commerce, and Commander John Bortniak, NOAA Corps (ret.); page 18b, courtesy of National Oceanic and Atmospheric Administration (NOAA)/ Department of Commerce, can NOAA Photo Library, NOAA Central Library, OAR/ERL/National Severe Storms Laboratory (NSSL)

Library of Congress Cataloging-in-Publication Data

Lilly, Melinda.
  Color / written by Melinda Lilly ; photos by Scott M. Thompson.
     p. cm. -- (Read and do science)
Summary: A simple description of what color is and what happens when different colors of light or paint are mixed. Includes bibliographical references and index.
  ISBN 1-58952-646-5 (hardcover)
  1. Color--Juvenile literature. [1. Color.]
I. Thompson, Scott M., ill. II. Title. III. Series.
  QC495.5.L55 2004
  535.6--dc22
                              2003012390
Printed in the USA

Table of Contents

Hide and Seek!

Where are the colors hiding?

They are hiding in the sunlight! Sunshine contains all the colors mixed together.

A rainbow, a **prism,** and a compact disc show white light separated into all its colors.

5

Primary Colors

A television or computer screen mixes red, blue, and green to make white light. Red, blue, and green are the **primary colors** of light.

By mixing different amounts of the primary colors, you can make all the other colors. Another thing that's special about primary colors is that you can't make them by mixing.

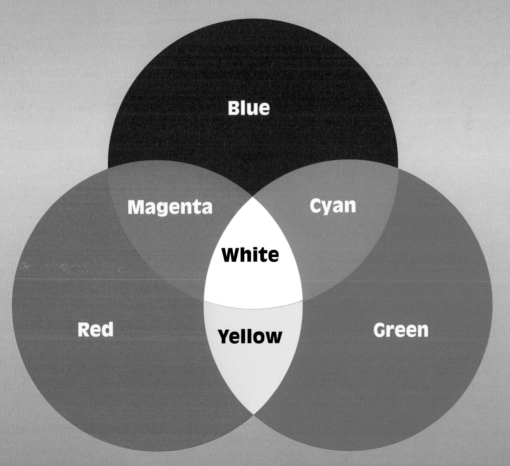

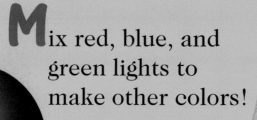

Mix red, blue, and green lights to make other colors!

Mixed-Up Light

What You Need:
- Three flashlights of equal strength
- Red, blue, and green **cellophane** (found at a gift-wrap store)
- Three rubber bands to fit around the ends of the flashlights
- A white wall or white paper
- Safety scissors
- A dark room

Cut a piece of each color of cellophane. Each piece must be big enough to wrap around the light end of a flashlight.

9

Make sure the flashlights are turned off. Wrap the green cellophane over the light end of one of the flashlights.

Secure it with a rubber band.

Put blue on the second flashlight and red on the third.

Shine the blue and red lights at the same spot on the white paper.

Blue + Red = Magenta

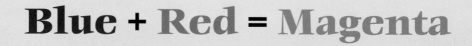

Magenta is a **secondary color** of light. It is made by mixing two primary colors.

Now mix the red and green lights. Surprise!

Red + Green = Yellow

Yellow is a secondary color of light.

Shine green and blue on the same spot. What color do you see?

Green + Blue = Cyan

Cyan is a secondary color of light.

Paint Colors

If you mix red and green paint, will you get yellow? No!

Pigment, such as paint and markers, mixes differently than light.

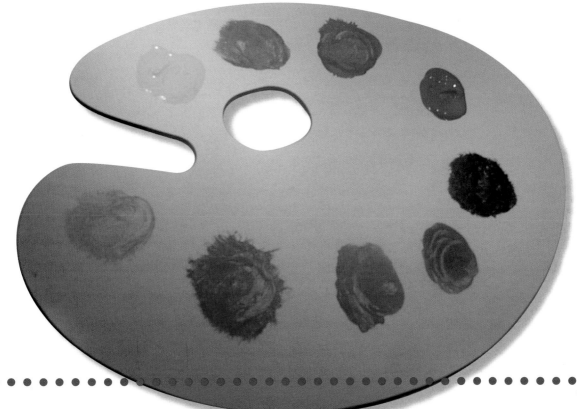

The primary colors of pigment are magenta, yellow, and cyan.

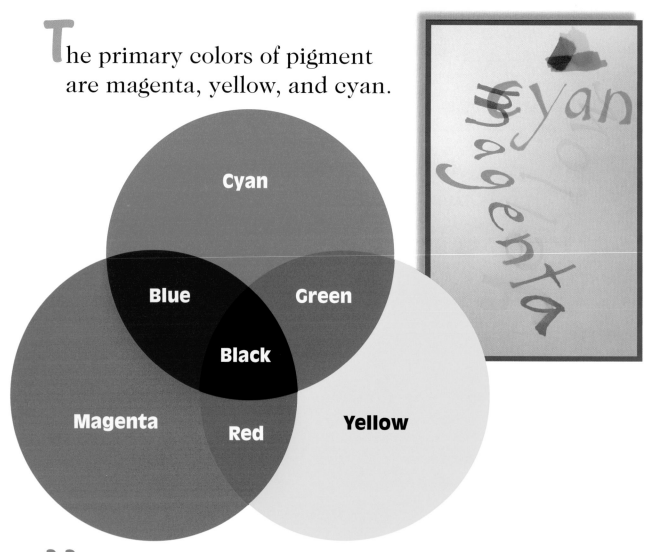

Hey, that looks familiar!

Here's How It Works

The primary colors of light are the secondary colors of pigment. The primary colors of pigment are the secondary colors of light.

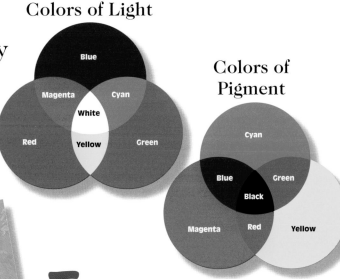

Colors of Light

Blue
Magenta · Cyan
White
Red · Yellow · Green

Colors of Pigment

Cyan
Blue · Green
Black
Magenta · Red · Yellow

To make other colors of pigment, you mix more or less of cyan, magenta and yellow. Mixing these three plus black and white made every color in this book.

What colors make up brown?

Hidden Colors

What You Need:

- Coffee-filter paper
- Brown water-soluble marker (markers made for children are water soluble)
- Bowl with 1/2 inch (1.3 cm) of water
- Two paper towels
- A clock

Use the marker to draw on the coffee filter. The area from the edge of the filter to one inch (2.6 cm) up should be kept blank.

Draw something that you won't miss. Your design will wash away during this activity.

Make a guess as to which colors mix to make the brown of the marker.

Cyan? Magenta?

Fold the colored filter so that the edges meet.

Put the filter in the bowl. The edges should sit in the water. The part with the design should be dry.

Over the next fifteen minutes the pigments will separate.

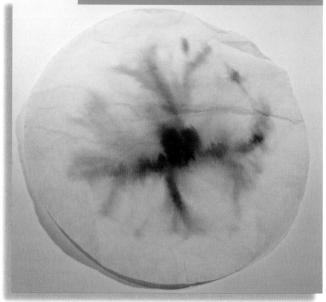

Shedding Light on Color

There are two types of color, those made entirely of light and those that use pigment.

Together, they make up all the colors we see!

Glossary

cellophane (SELL oh fayn) — a protective wrap for food

cyan (SYE an) — green blue

magenta (muh JEN tuh) — purple red

pigment (PIG munt) — color in paint, ink, hair, skin, fur, plants, and more

prism (PRIZ em) — a shape made of plastic or glass that can separate white light

primary colors (PRY mer ee KUL urz) — the colors that can be mixed to make all other colors

secure (sih KUER) — to fasten something that is loose in order to hold it down

secondary color (SEK on der ee KUL ur) — A color made by mixing two primary colors in equal amounts

Take It Further: Melting Colors

1. Pour water into three or more glasses.

2. Put a different color of food coloring into each glass of water.

3. Pour each type of colored water into a balloon by using a funnel.

4. Freeze the balloons.

5. Put the balloons in a big bowl or a few tubs.

6. Mix together the colors as they melt.

Think About It!

1. People used to say the primary colors of pigment were red, blue, and yellow. How is magenta like red? How is cyan like blue?

2. If you mixed together the colors of the rainbow, what color would you get?

3. If you wanted to make orange paint, what two colors would you mix together?

Index